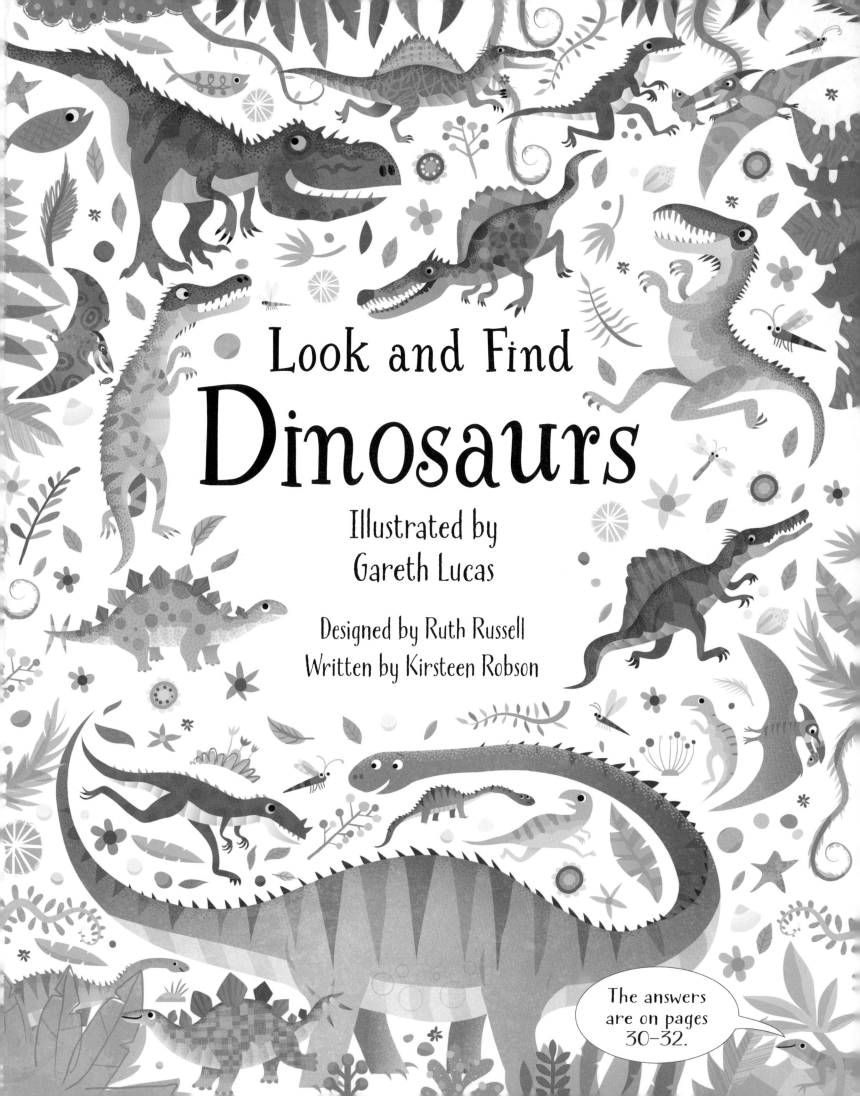

Look and Find
Dinosaurs

Illustrated by
Gareth Lucas

Designed by Ruth Russell
Written by Kirsteen Robson

The answers are on pages 30-32.

5

16

ANSWERS

Cover

1

2-3

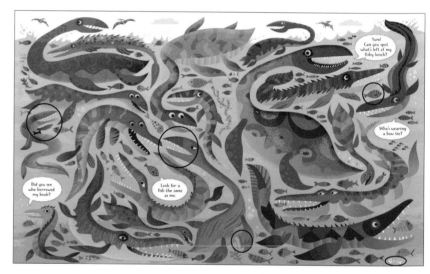

4-5

3 have caught a fish.

6-7

8-9

10–11

12–13

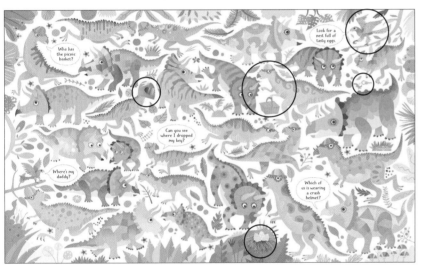

14–15

16–17

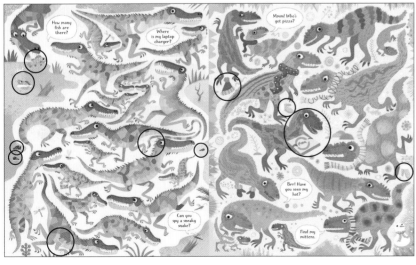

There are 5 fish.

18–19

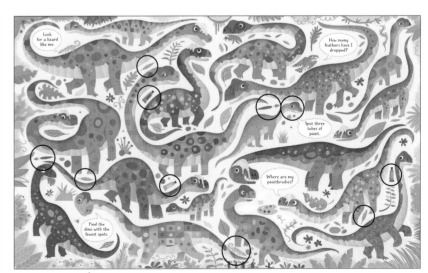

There are 3 dropped feathers.

20–21

31

ANSWERS (continued)

22-23

24-25

26-27

There are 9 blue flowers.

28-29